SOCCER
SUPERSTARS

CARLTON KIDS

THIS IS A CARLTON BOOK

Text, design, and illustration © Carlton Books Limited 2018
This edition published in 2018 by Carlton Books Limited,
an imprint of the Carlton Publishing Group,
20 Mortimer Street, London W1T 3JW

Written by Emily Stead

A catalogue record for this book is available
from the British Library.

ISBN: 978-1-78312-409-1

Printed in China
10 9 8 7 6 5 4 3 2 1

Consultant: Anthony Hobbs
Executive Editor: Bryony Davies
Design Manager: Luke Griffin
Design: RockJaw Creative
Production: Nicola Davey

Special thanks to John Ashley

CONTENTS

Note to readers: the facts and statistics in this book are accurate as of February 25, 2018.

STARS OF THE GAME

Welcome to **SOCCER SUPERSTARS**, a celebration of the hottest players in world soccer right now. This collection features **18 LEGENDS OF THE GAME**, from superb keepers to explosive strikers—there's no one you wouldn't want in your squad.

Learn how each player started out, his skills, clubs, and how his talent took him to the top. Plus find out all the **FACTS AND STATS** to wow your friends. A chapter on the young stars currently taking the game by storm completes our collection. Pick your tip for a future Ballon d'Or winner, then tackle our **FIENDISH QUIZ** to test your knowledge of all the pro players.

PLAYERS AND STATS

The player profiles give you the lowdown on each player's career so far—appearances, goals, and trophies won. Whose trophy cabinet is bulging the most? Which players have scored season after season, made the most assists, or set special records? Compare the stats and choose your first XI.

Real Madrid legends Toni Kroos, Marcelo, and Sergio Ramos celebrate another goal for Los Blancos (the Whites: the team's nickname).

SUPERSTARS DREAM TEAM

While reading this book, think about which players would make it into your dream team. Fill in the players' names on the left and put them in position on the pitch.

PLAYER NAME	SHIRT
	◯
	◯
	◯
	◯
	◯
	◯
	◯
	◯
	◯
	◯
	◯

LEONARDO BONUCCI

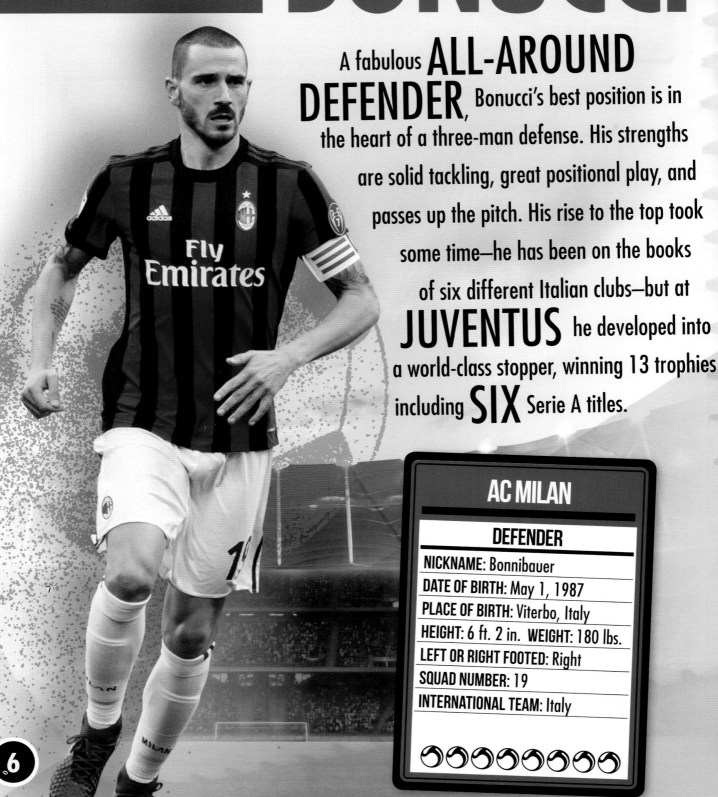

A fabulous **ALL-AROUND DEFENDER**, Bonucci's best position is in the heart of a three-man defense. His strengths are solid tackling, great positional play, and passes up the pitch. His rise to the top took some time—he has been on the books of six different Italian clubs—but at **JUVENTUS** he developed into a world-class stopper, winning 13 trophies including **SIX** Serie A titles.

AC MILAN

DEFENDER

NICKNAME:	Bonnibauer
DATE OF BIRTH:	May 1, 1987
PLACE OF BIRTH:	Viterbo, Italy
HEIGHT: 6 ft. 2 in.	**WEIGHT:** 180 lbs.
LEFT OR RIGHT FOOTED:	Right
SQUAD NUMBER:	19
INTERNATIONAL TEAM:	Italy

CLUBS						
	INTERNAZIONALE	TREVISO	PISA	BARI	JUVENTUS	AC MILAN
	Caps 4	Caps 41	Caps 18	Caps 39	Caps 319	Caps 30
	Goals 0	Goals 4	Goals 1	Goals 1	Goals 19	Goals 1

TROPHIES			
7 Serie A	**3** Italian Cup	**3** Italian Super Cup

GOLDEN YEARS

When Juventus bought Bonucci in the summer of 2010, it was the start of something special. He went straight into the side alongside Italy teammate Giorgio Chiellini. He and Chiellini later partnered with Andrea Barzagli, forming a trio at the back nicknamed "BBC." Six Italian league titles were won in a row, along with three Italian Cups. Bonucci also reached two UEFA Champions League finals, but was on the losing side both times, to Barcelona in 2015 and Real Madrid in 2017. In 2016 he was voted Italy's soccer player of the year and named in the UEFA Team of the Year.

ITALY INTERNATIONAL

With 75 caps and five goals for his country, Bonucci's international career has had many highs and lows. He was first called up in March 2010 and made the World Cup squad, but was an unused substitute as Italy was knocked out in the first round. Two years later it was a different story—Bonucci started in all but one match as Italy reached the final of EURO 2012, losing 4–0 to Spain. Another miserable World Cup followed in 2014, though Bonucci was made captain following the tournament. Sadly for the defender, Italy did not qualify for the 2018 World Cup, losing in a play-off match to Sweden.

MILAN MOVE

When Bonucci moved to Juve's rival AC Milan in the summer of 2017, it was one of the most surprising transfers of recent seasons. He left a team that had twice finished runner-up in the UEFA Champions League to join a club that hadn't even qualified for that season's tournament. Milan paid around $45 million for the 30-year-old and made him their captain. While Bonucci has had a rocky start at Milan so far, don't bet against this determined defender coming back even stronger.

Bonucci is a leader on the pitch for club and country.

GAME FACT >>>>>>

Bonucci broke his nose after only 30 seconds in Italy's World Cup play-off match against Sweden in 2017. Incredibly, he managed to play on for the entire match!

KEVIN DE BRUYNE

In Manchester City, **MIDFIELD MAESTRO** Kevin De Bruyne has finally found a club to call home. He was signed for a reported fee of over $80 million in August 2015 and has been in **STUNNING FORM** ever since. 2017 saw him nominated for the prized **BALLON D'OR** award for the third year in a row.

MANCHESTER CITY

MIDFIELDER

NICKNAMES:	The Ginger Pelé, KDB
DATE OF BIRTH:	June 28, 1991
PLACE OF BIRTH:	Ghent, Belgium
HEIGHT: 5 ft. 11 in.	**WEIGHT:** 149 lbs.
LEFT OR RIGHT FOOTED:	Left
SQUAD NUMBER:	17
INTERNATIONAL TEAM:	Belgium

CLUBS	GENK	CHELSEA	WERDER BREMEN	VFL WOLFSBURG	MANCHESTER CITY
	Caps 113 Goals 17	Caps 9 Goals 0	Caps 34 Goals 10	Caps 72 Goals 20	Caps 125 Goals 34
TROPHIES	2 English League Cup	1 German Cup	1 German Super Cup	1 Belgian Pro League	1 Belgian Cup

GROWING UP

Kevin De Bruyne's childhood had an international flavor—his mother was born in Burundi, his father is Belgian, and he traveled regularly between England and Africa. De Bruyne eventually settled on Belgium as his national team. His first senior appearance was for Belgian club Genk in 2009, where he played a key role in the club's title-winning side, making 17 assists and scoring six goals from the heart of midfield. A move to London followed in January 2012 when Chelsea signed De Bruyne, but loaned him straight back to Genk.

GERMAN GIANT

At the start of the 2012–13 season De Bruyne switched to the Bundesliga, joining German club Werder Bremen on a season-long loan. After a successful campaign, he returned to parent club Chelsea, but could not get into the first team. Desperate for game time, De Bruyne signed for Wolfsburg in a $27 million permanent move. He made a huge impact, providing a record-breaking number of assists for the club as Wolfsburg finished as runner-up in the league and as German Cup winner. It was only a matter of time before a bigger club came calling for Germany's Soccer Player of the Year in 2015.

CITY SLICKER

De Bruyne joined Manchester City in August 2015 for a club record fee, and has been a standout performer in City's first XI, contributing 34 goals and over 50 assists in his first 125 appearances in all competitions. Kevin has confessed that he actually prefers to create goals for his teammates rather than score them! Along with his creativity and defense splitting passes, De Bruyne's reputation for hard work saw him quickly become a crowd favorite. He is now playing the best soccer of his career and is a key man for the free-scoring Sky Blues.

De Bruyne cemented his place as a regular for Belgium during the 2018 FIFA World Cup qualifiers.

GAME FACT ≫≫≫≫≫

As befits a player with an international childhood, Kevin is fluent in Dutch, French, and English.

EDEN HAZARD

Chelsea's **BELGIAN ACE** in midfield, Hazard has flair and pace. His six seasons at Stamford Bridge have seen him mature into one of the finest players in the world, often compared to Messi and Ronaldo. A **SUPERB PASSER**, Hazard can operate on either wing or in central midfield, thanks to his skill with **BOTH FEET**. He's claimed three league titles, and the UEFA Champions League and the Ballon d'Or are his next goals.

CHELSEA

ATTACKING MIDFIELDER

FULL NAME:	Eden Michael Hazard
NICKNAME:	N/A
DATE OF BIRTH:	January 7, 1991
PLACE OF BIRTH:	La Louvière, Belgium
HEIGHT: 5 ft. 8 in.	**WEIGHT:** 167 lbs.
LEFT OR RIGHT FOOTED:	Both
SQUAD NUMBER:	10
INTERNATIONAL TEAM:	Belgium

CLUBS		
LILLE		**CHELSEA**
Caps 194 Goals 50		Caps 284 Goals 87

TROPHIES				
2 Premier League	**1** English League Cup	**1** Ligue 1	**1** French Cup	**1** UEFA Europa League

FRENCH CONNECTION

Hazard joined French Ligue 1 club Lille's academy at the age of 14. The young star became a permanent member of the first team soon after making his pro debut, aged just 16, and quickly made a big impact in midfield. He was named France's Young Player of the Year twice in a row, in 2009 and 2010, becoming the first non-French player to win the award. Fast and technically gifted, Hazard played almost 200 times for Lille, scoring 50 goals. His finest season was in 2010–11, when Lille won a league and cup double.

HERO HAZARD

With the world at his feet, Hazard signed for Chelsea aged 21 for a fee of around $44 million in summer 2012. His first season ended with him scoring 13 goals in all competitions. With some first-class performances under José Mourinho, by May 2015 Hazard had been voted Chelsea's Player of the Year two seasons running as the Blues ran away with the Premier League title and won the League Cup. In 2016–17 Chelsea was crowned champion and Hazard was the hero once again.

YOUNG SKIPPER

Hazard won his first cap for Belgium aged 17, but had to wait three years to score his first international goal. He has since played over 80 times for the Red Devils, and scored over 20 goals. Belgium's star-studded golden generation reached the quarterfinals of both the 2014 World Cup and EURO 2016. With Hazard wearing the captain's armband, Belgium is an organized and dangerous side.

Thanks to his years at Lille, Hazard was eligible to play for France, but he chose his home country instead.

GAME FACT ›››››

Belgium once banned Hazard for three matches after he left a EURO 2012 qualifier early to go for a burger after having being subbed. Now he follows a much healthier diet!

ANDRÉS INIESTA

The **MAGICAL MIDFIELDER** has won every honor in the game, including eight Spanish league titles and four UEFA Champions Leagues. Iniesta was the **DRIVING FORCE** behind Spain's recent dominance in international soccer, winning the EUROs twice and the **WORLD CUP** in 2010. He is probably the **BEST PLAYER** never to have won the Ballon d'Or.

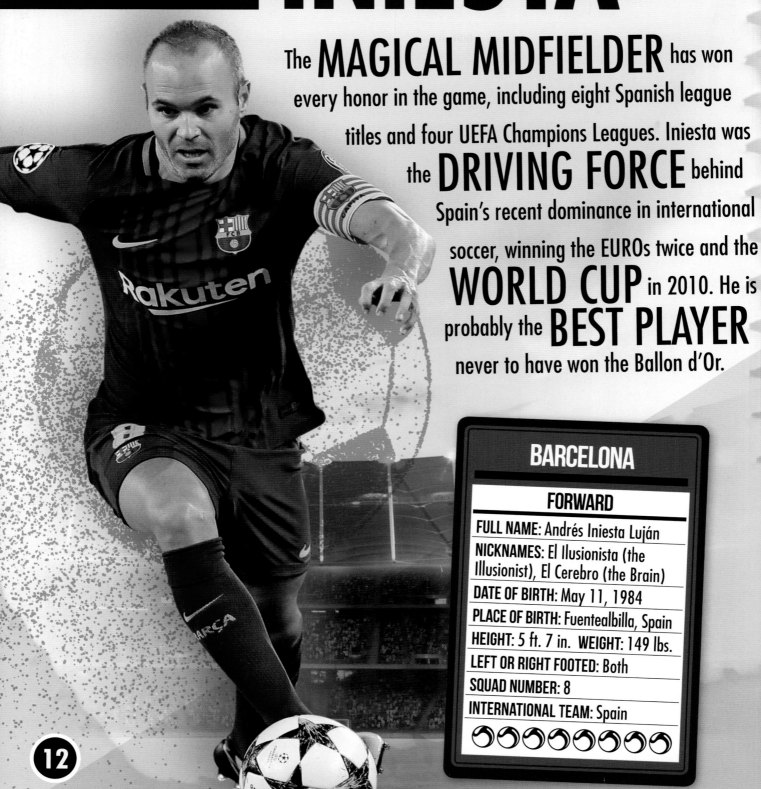

BARCELONA

FORWARD

FULL NAME: Andrés Iniesta Luján

NICKNAMES: El Ilusionista (the Illusionist), El Cerebro (the Brain)

DATE OF BIRTH: May 11, 1984

PLACE OF BIRTH: Fuentealbilla, Spain

HEIGHT: 5 ft. 7 in.   **WEIGHT:** 149 lbs.

LEFT OR RIGHT FOOTED: Both

SQUAD NUMBER: 8

INTERNATIONAL TEAM: Spain

CLUBS

BARCELONA B	BARCELONA
Caps 54 Goals 5	Caps 657 Goals 56

TROPHIES

4 UEFA Champions League	**5** Spanish Cup	**3** FIFA Club World Cup	**1** FIFA World Cup	**2** UEFA European Championship
8 La Liga	**6** Spanish Super Cup	**3** UEFA Super Cup		

LEAVING HOME

Iniesta was just 10 years old and playing for his local club Albacete's youth team when he caught the eye of the Barcelona scouts. He was invited to join Barça's famous La Masia academy aged 12, and left his family and village to follow his dream. A shy boy, Iniesta had to overcome homesickness, but by the age of 15, he had been made Barcelona's U15 captain and was showing skills beyond his years. The then first-team captain Pep Guardiola predicted that the young Iniesta would take his position one day—and he was right!

SPARKLING SPANIARD

Iniesta was a key man as Spain sparkled between 2008 and 2012, twice winning the European Championship as well as the World Cup in 2010. Iniesta scored the extra-time winner in the 2010 World Cup final against the Netherlands to clinch the trophy for the first time in Spain's history. His exceptional creative passing and goals also saw him named Player of the Tournament at EURO 2012. Iniesta joined Spain's 100-cap club at the 2014 World Cup.

Andrés Iniesta—one of Spain's greatest ever players.

ONE-CLUB MAN

Iniesta made his first-team debut for Barcelona in October 2002, the first of more than an incredible 650 appearances for the club so far. His trophy cabinet is pretty special—he's won an impressive eight La Liga titles and the UEFA Champions League four times. Iniesta has captained the side since 2015 and shares the club record of winning 30 trophies with Lionel Messi. He has signed a lifetime contract with the La Liga giants and intends to finish his career with the club.

GAME FACT ≫≫≫≫≫

Iniesta is a co-owner of Albacete Balompié, his old youth team, and also owns a vineyard in the village where he grew up.

HARRY KANE

Harry Kane has developed into a **SUPERSTAR STRIKER**, with a lethal touch in front of goal and an excellent scoring record. When Kane gets on a hot streak there's almost no defense that can stop him! His **SUPERB FINISHING** ability, brilliant holdup play, and close control mean he can also play as a lone striker. He's a **TRULY GREAT** goal scorer.

TOTTENHAM HOTSPUR

FORWARD

FULL NAME: Harry Edward Kane
NICKNAME: The Hurrikane
DATE OF BIRTH: July 28, 1993
PLACE OF BIRTH: London, England
HEIGHT: 6 ft. 2 in. **WEIGHT:** 189 lbs.
LEFT OR RIGHT FOOTED: Right
SQUAD NUMBER: 10
INTERNATIONAL TEAM: England

STAT ATTACK

CLUBS

LEYTON ORIENT (LOAN)	MILLWALL (LOAN)	NORWICH CITY (LOAN)	LEICESTER CITY (LOAN)	TOTTENHAM HOTSPUR
Caps 18 Goals 5	Caps 27 Goals 9	Caps 5 Goals 0	Caps 15 Goals 2	Caps 199 Goals 132

KANE SCORED 56 GOALS FOR CLUB AND COUNTRY IN 2017— MORE THAN ANY OTHER PLAYER IN EUROPE'S TOP FIVE LEAGUES.

SHARPSHOOTER

Kane joined Tottenham aged 11. His breakthrough came in 2014–15 when he smashed home 21 goals in 34 league games for Spurs. The following season Harry claimed his first Premier League Golden Boot with 25 league goals from 38 topflight appearances. Despite missing 11 weeks of the 2016–17 season through injury, Kane hit another 29 league goals from just 30 games to win his second Golden Boot. He has his eye on Alan Shearer's all-time Premier League goal record of 260 and, still in his mid-twenties, he has time on his side in the battle of the goal kings.

LEADING THE LINE

Kane is England's main man up front. With an international scoring record of a goal every two matches, Kane will be keen to add to his tally as he continues playing for England. Kane made his England debut in March 2015 and was part of the squad for EURO 2016. When he captained the side for the first time in a World Cup qualifier against Scotland, it was a boyhood dream come true for Harry.

LOAN RANGER

In a bid to kickstart his career, Spurs loaned Kane to Leyton Orient, Millwall, Norwich, and Leicester, but he never made a major impact at any of these clubs. Some critics claimed that Kane was not cut out to play at the highest level, but he worked hard to prove them wrong. An old-fashioned number 10, Kane has a real passion for the game and loves nothing better than scoring goals. Harry improved his strength and physique to earn his first start under manager Mauricio Pochettino. The rest is history!

Kane has made over 20 appearances for his country and is an England regular.

GAME FACT >>>>>>

Kane was once a member of Arsenal's youth academy, but was let go by the Gunners after only one season.

TONI KROOS

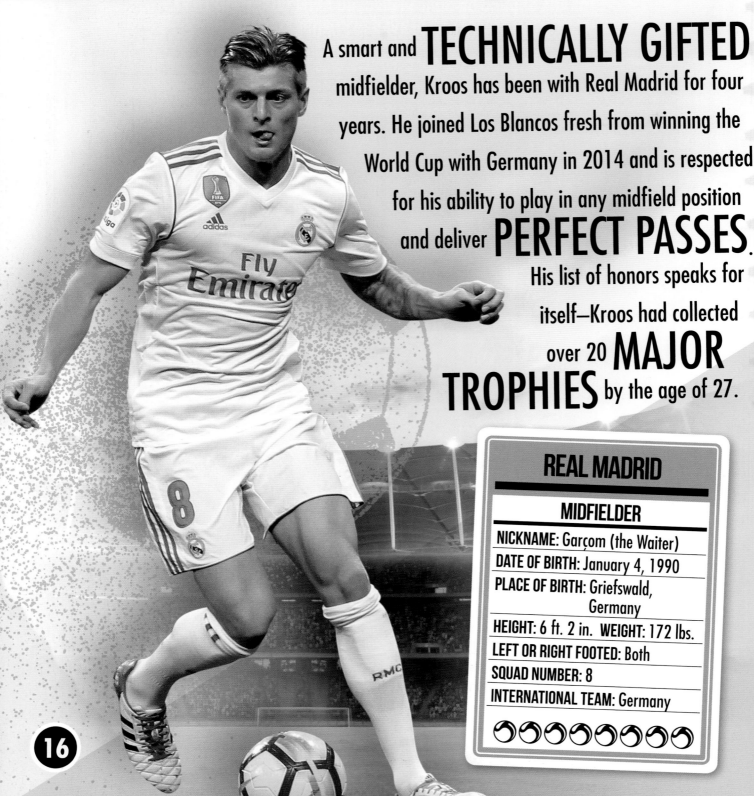

A smart and **TECHNICALLY GIFTED** midfielder, Kroos has been with Real Madrid for four years. He joined Los Blancos fresh from winning the World Cup with Germany in 2014 and is respected for his ability to play in any midfield position and deliver **PERFECT PASSES**. His list of honors speaks for itself—Kroos had collected over 20 **MAJOR TROPHIES** by the age of 27.

REAL MADRID

MIDFIELDER

NICKNAME: Garçom (the Waiter)

DATE OF BIRTH: January 4, 1990

PLACE OF BIRTH: Griefswald, Germany

HEIGHT: 6 ft. 2 in. **WEIGHT:** 172 lbs.

LEFT OR RIGHT FOOTED: Both

SQUAD NUMBER: 8

INTERNATIONAL TEAM: Germany

STAT ATTACK

CLUBS

BAYERN MUNICH II	BAYERN MUNICH	BAYER LEVERKUSEN (LOAN)	REAL MADRID
Caps 13 Goals 4	Caps 205 Goals 25	Caps 48 Goals 10	Caps 176 Goals 11

TROPHIES

3 UEFA Champions League	**3** German Cup	**1** La Liga	**3** FIFA Club World Cup	**1** FIFA World Cup
3 Bundesliga	**1** German Super Cup	**1** Spanish Super Cup	**4** UEFA Super Cup	

KROOS CONTROL

Kroos was called up to Bayern's first-team squad aged 17. At the time of his debut, he was the youngest player ever to represent Bayern in a pro match. A successful loan spell at Bayer Leverkusen from 2009 to 2010 saw Kroos play 48 matches for the side. He ended his time there with ten goals and a strong assists record. On his return to Munich in summer 2010, Kroos quickly became a first-team regular, winning three Bundesliga titles and a UEFA Champions League medal in 2013, although injury ruled him out of the final. His accurate passing and set-piece play gives Kroos the ability to control matches from midfield.

WORLD CUP WONDER

In 2010, aged 20, Kroos broke into Germany's senior squad. He made the World Cup squad that year, as Germany reached the semifinals in South Africa, but it was at the 2014 World Cup in Brazil that Kroos really raised his game. His man-of-the-match performances, two goals, and four assists helped Germany win the World Cup for a fourth time. Kroos was unlucky to miss out on the Golden Ball for the best player of the tournament, which went to Lionel Messi. Some experts believe that Kroos is Germany's most important player.

GERMAN GALÁCTICO

Kroos went in search of more silverware following his sparkling World Cup displays in a move to Real Madrid. Real paid a fee of $27–35 million in the summer of 2014. While he didn't light up the Bernabéu in his first couple of seasons, Kroos has found his best form since—he's known as a masterful midfielder with a pinpoint passing range. Toni has won the UEFA Champions League twice and the Spanish league title once with Real. He is the only German player to have lifted the Champions League trophy with two different clubs.

Kroos in action in an international friendly against France, in November 2017.

GAME FACT ≫≫≫≫

Kroos is the first soccer player born in the former East Germany to have won the World Cup.

17

ROBERT LEWANDOWSKI

A **FANTASTIC FINISHER**, Bayern Munich's star striker is also captain of Poland. He is hailed as Poland's **GREATEST PLAYER** of all time, thanks to his glorious goal record, work rate, and leadership on the pitch. He **EXPLODED** onto the scene and scored 100 German topflight goals faster than any player from outside Germany. It's no wonder he's valued at a cool $130 million!

BAYERN MUNICH

FORWARD

NICKNAME: The Body	
DATE OF BIRTH: August 21, 1988	
PLACE OF BIRTH: Warsaw, Poland	
HEIGHT: 6 ft. 3 in.	**WEIGHT:** 174 lbs.
LEFT OR RIGHT FOOTED: Right	
SQUAD NUMBER: 9	
INTERNATIONAL TEAM: Poland	

CLUBS			
ZNICZ PRUSZKÓW	LECH POZNAŃ	BORUSSIA DORTMUND	BAYERN MUNICH
Caps 63 Goals 37	Caps 82 Goals 41	Caps 187 Goals 103	Caps 178 Goals 136

TROPHIES	**5** Bundesliga	**2** German Cup	**3** German Super Cup	**1** Polish League	**1** Polish Cup	**1** Polish Super Cup

A TASTE FOR GOALS

Robert kicked off his club career with Znicz Pruszków in the Polish third division. His 15 goals helped Znicz win promotion and the following season Lewandowski scored 21 goals in the second tier. In June 2008, the striker switched sides to topflight side Lech Poznań, scoring on his debut. He was the league's top scorer in 2009–10 with 18 goals and led Lech to the title. His goal scoring form while playing in Poland was red-hot, earning Lewandowski a transfer to German club Borussia Dortmund in the summer of 2010. The move didn't disrupt his form, and his scoring streak continued in the Bundesliga and in European competition.

ROB'S RECORDS

Lewandowski spent four seasons with Dortmund, scoring over 100 goals in fewer than 200 appearances. His 74 league goals were key to the club becoming German champion twice. In January 2014 however, the striker left for Bayern Munich on a free transfer. Robert continued his brilliant career there, winning the league title three times as well as one German Cup and two Super Cups. He once scored five goals for Bayern despite only playing the second half—talk about a super sub! He also recorded the fastest Bundesliga hat trick (3 minutes 22 seconds) as part of his five-goal haul.

POLE SCORER

Robert's debut for the national team came in September 2008, just after his 20th birthday. He came off the bench to score his first goal for Poland. EURO 2012 was Lewandowski's first major international tournament, and while the Eagles crashed out early on, the striker played in every game, scoring once. By 2014 he was captain of Poland and a regular goal scorer for his country. In World Cup qualification in 2017, Lewandowski moved on to 50 goals, as Poland topped their group. Russia 2018 was Poland's first appearance at the tournament for 12 years, with Lewandowski's goals in qualifying key to this achievement.

Lewandowski scored an amazing 16 goals in qualifying for the 2018 World Cup, a European record.

GAME FACT >>>>>>

Robert comes from a sporting family—his father was a Polish judo champion and soccer player, and his mother and sister have been professional volleyball players.

MARCELO

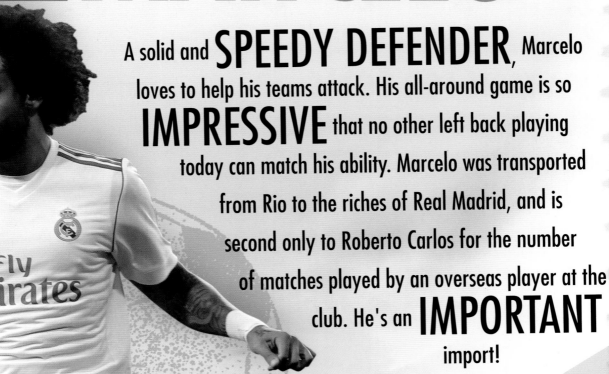

A solid and **SPEEDY DEFENDER**, Marcelo loves to help his teams attack. His all-around game is so **IMPRESSIVE** that no other left back playing today can match his ability. Marcelo was transported from Rio to the riches of Real Madrid, and is second only to Roberto Carlos for the number of matches played by an overseas player at the club. He's an **IMPORTANT** import!

REAL MADRID	
DEFENDER	
FULL NAME: Marcelo Vieira da Silva Júnior	
NICKNAME: El Loco (the Crazy)	
DATE OF BIRTH: May 12, 1988	
PLACE OF BIRTH: Rio de Janeiro, Brazil	
HEIGHT: 5 ft. 8 in.	**WEIGHT:** 176 lbs.
LEFT OR RIGHT FOOTED: Left	
SQUAD NUMBER: 12	
INTERNATIONAL TEAM: Brazil	

STAT ATTACK

CLUBS

FLUMINENSE	REAL MADRID
Caps 30 Goals 6	Caps 437 Goals 31

TROPHIES

3 UEFA Champions League	**2** Spanish Cup	**3** UEFA Super Cup	**1** Olympic Silver Medal	**1** Olympic Bronze Medal
4 La Liga	**3** Spanish Super Cup	**3** FIFA Club World Cup	**1** FIFA Confederations Cup	

BRAZILIAN BORN

Marcelo grew up in a poor area of Rio de Janeiro in Brazil. His father was a firefighter and his mother a teacher, but Marcelo had no wish to follow in their footsteps—all he wanted to do was play soccer. Playing a mix of street soccer and futsal at the beach helped Marcelo develop his skills, and he signed for Fluminense's youth side aged 13. Marcelo became known as a fast, attacking, and hardworking fullback. When Real Madrid's scouts watched him play in 2007, half of Europe's top clubs wanted him, but Real won his signature and Marcelo arrived in Spain in the January transfer window.

SAMBA STYLE

Marcelo has won almost 50 caps for Brazil and scored six goals, playing for his country for over a decade. He has won two Olympic medals—a bronze in 2008 and a silver in 2012—as well as the 2013 FIFA Confederations Cup. When Brazil lost to Germany in a crushing 7–1 semifinal defeat at the World Cup in 2014, Marcelo called it the worst day of his career. Four years on, the defender is in the form of his life.

Marcelo is often compared to Roberto Carlos, another legendary Brazilian left back. Many experts say Marcelo is even better!

REAL WINNER

Marcelo made Madrid's first 11 straightaway at left back. But after a couple of poor seasons playing out of position, Marcelo's breakthrough came in 2010–11. New manager José Mourinho returned him to left back and, by the end of that season, some said he was as valuable as Ronaldo and Messi. As the 2016–17 season ended, Marcelo had won 18 major trophies with Real Madrid, including four La Liga titles and a treble of UEFA Champions League wins, all before the age of 30.

GAME FACT »»»»»

Marcelo's best friends in soccer are his Real Madrid teammate Cristiano Ronaldo and the Brazil defender Pepe.

LIONEL MESSI

In a world of soccer superstars, mini **MAGICIAN** Messi is a megastar. He's been at the top of his game since debuting for Barcelona in 2004, and will go down in history as one of soccer's all-time greats. His silverware collection is **SECOND TO NONE**, with four UEFA Champions League titles and eight La Liga trophies. He's a deadly dribbler with a **LETHAL LEFT FOOT** and scores goals for fun for both Barcelona and Argentina.

BARCELONA

FORWARD

FULL NAME:	Lionel Andrés Messi Cuccittini
NICKNAME:	La Pulga (the Flea)
DATE OF BIRTH:	June 24, 1987
PLACE OF BIRTH:	Rosario, Argentina
HEIGHT: 5 ft. 7 in.	**WEIGHT:** 158 lbs.
LEFT OR RIGHT FOOTED:	Left
SQUAD NUMBER:	10
INTERNATIONAL TEAM:	Argentina

STAT ATTACK

CLUBS

BARCELONA C	BARCELONA B	BARCELONA
Caps 10 Goals 5	Caps 22 Goals 6	Caps 619 Goals 534

TROPHIES

4 UEFA Champions League	**5** Spanish Cup	**3** UEFA Super Cup	**3** FIFA Club World Cup	**1** Olympic Gold Medal
8 La Liga	**7** Spanish Super Cup			

STAR QUALITY

Growing up in Argentina, Messi started playing soccer from an early age. He was always smaller than his teammates, but that didn't stop him. At the age of ten, he was told that his body was not growing normally and he needed medical treatment. Barcelona agreed to pay for his treatment and Messi moved with his family to Spain. By the age of 14, Messi was part of Barcelona's greatest ever youth side and his talent was clear to everyone who saw him play. Messi played his first game for Barça's senior side, a friendly in late 2003, aged just 16 years and four months.

REAL RIVALRY

The best player in Barcelona's history? His individual records are too long to list, but Messi is responsible for much of Barcelona's spectacular success in recent years. He has broken almost every club and La Liga record going, winning four UEFA Champions Leagues and 30 trophies overall with the Catalan club. A fifth Champions League win would make Messi the most successful non-European player in the competition's history. Messi's greatest rival is Real Madrid's Cristiano Ronaldo. The pair have battled it out between them to win the Ballon d'Or trophy five times each in the last ten years.

AWESOME ARGENTINE

While Messi has won trophy after trophy at Barcelona, his Argentina side has not been so successful. Messi has been on the losing side with Argentina in four major finals, going out on penalties twice. He even retired for a while following the 2016 loss to Chile in the Copa América! His only senior trophy won with his country was a gold medal at the 2008 Olympic Games.

Messi is Argentina's top scorer of all time, with 61 goals by the end of qualification for Russia 2018.

GAME FACT >>>>>

In 2012, Messi scored an unbelievable 91 goals combined in all competitions for Barcelona and Argentina. What a record!

MANUEL NEUER

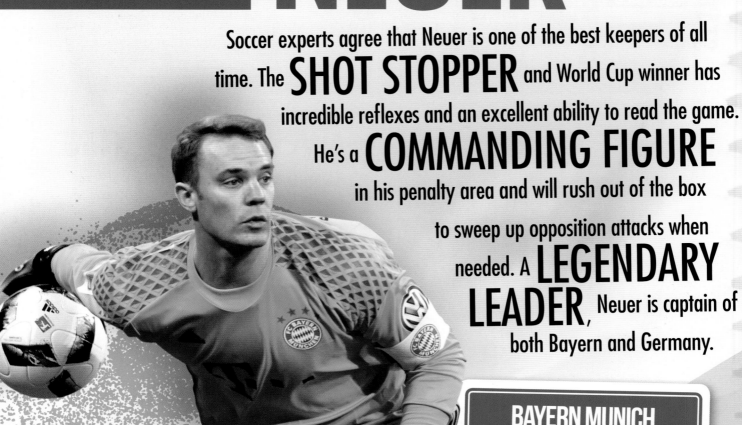

Soccer experts agree that Neuer is one of the best keepers of all time. The **SHOT STOPPER** and World Cup winner has incredible reflexes and an excellent ability to read the game. He's a **COMMANDING FIGURE** in his penalty area and will rush out of the box to sweep up opposition attacks when needed. A **LEGENDARY LEADER**, Neuer is captain of both Bayern and Germany.

BAYERN MUNICH

GOALKEEPER

FULL NAME:	Manuel Peter Neuer
NICKNAMES:	Snapper, Manu
DATE OF BIRTH:	March 27, 1986
PLACE OF BIRTH:	Gelsenkirchen, West Germany
HEIGHT: 6 ft. 3 in.	**WEIGHT:** 202 lbs.
LEFT OR RIGHT FOOTED:	Right
SQUAD NUMBER:	1
INTERNATIONAL TEAM:	Germany

STAT ATTACK

CLUBS

SCHALKE 04 II	SCHALKE 04	BAYERN MUNICH
Caps 29 Goals 0	Caps 203 Goals 0	Caps 299 Goals 0

TROPHIES

1 UEFA Champions League
5 Bundesliga
4 German Cup
1 FIFA Club World Cup
1 FIFA World Cup

1 German League Cup
2 German Super Cup
1 UEFA Super Cup

SCHALKE START

Manuel started playing soccer when he was four and later joined his hometown club, Schalke 04. At first he played outfield, but wanted to copy his idol Jens Lehmann and so he became a goalkeeper. He started out with the club's second team in the 2003–04 season, but by 2006–07 had become a first-team regular. Brilliant at commanding his defense and a standout shot shopper, Neuer helped Schalke win two trophies. At the end of the 2010–11 season, Schalke reached the UEFA Champions League semifinals, but lost to Manchester United. Hungry for success, Neuer announced he was moving to the rival Bayern Munich.

WORLD CUP WINNER

Manuel made his international debut in 2009 and was first-choice keeper for the 2010 World Cup, when Germany reached the semifinals. The 2014 World Cup was the highlight of Neuer's international career so far. Playing as a "sweeper-keeper," he helped Germany attack further up the pitch. A shutout in the final saw Germany beat Argentina to take the trophy, and Neuer was awarded the Golden Glove for the best goalkeeper in the tournament. That year, he finished third in the Ballon d'Or voting, behind Messi and Ronaldo.

BAYERN'S BEST

In his first season at Bayern, Neuer went 1,000 minutes without conceding a goal, breaking the club record for the most competitive shutouts in a row. His reputation grew following the UEFA Champions League final in 2012 when Neuer scored in the penalty shoot-out, but ultimately lost to Chelsea. A year later, Bayern was back in the Champions League final, and this time it beat Borussia Dortmund. Neuer and Bayern went on to dominate German soccer, winning a record-breaking five Bundesliga titles in a row, with league and cup doubles in 2012–13, 2013–14, and 2015–16.

Neuer has been voted the World's Best Goalkeeper and UEFA Goalkeeper of the Year eight times altogether.

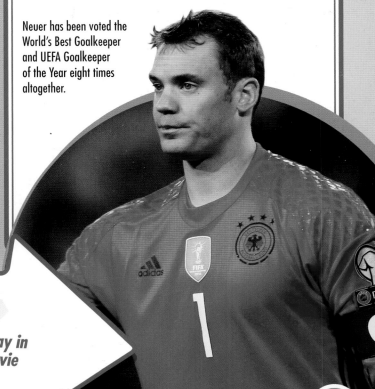

GAME FACT ⟩⟩⟩⟩⟩

Neuer was the voice for character Frank McCay in the German version of the 2013 animated movie Monsters University—strange but true!

NEYMAR

From playing barefoot on the backstreets of São Paulo to his $263 million **WORLD-RECORD TRANSFER** to Paris Saint-Germain, Neymar's journey to soccer stardom has been nothing short of incredible. The **BOY FROM BRAZIL** has established himself as one of the game's brightest stars, winning a host of trophies for **CLUB AND COUNTRY**.

PARIS SAINT-GERMAIN

FORWARD
FULL NAME: Neymar da Silva Santos Júnior
NICKNAMES: O Joia (the Gem), NJR
DATE OF BIRTH: February 5, 1992
PLACE OF BIRTH: São Paulo, Brazil
HEIGHT: 5 ft. 9 in. **WEIGHT:** 149 lbs.
LEFT OR RIGHT FOOTED: Both
SQUAD NUMBER: 10
INTERNATIONAL TEAM: Brazil

STAT ATTACK

CLUBS			
SANTOS	**BARCELONA**	**PARIS SAINT-GERMAIN**	
Caps 223 Goals 136	Caps 186 Goals 105	Caps 28 Goals 28	

TROPHIES					
1 UEFA Champions League	**3** Spanish Cup	**1** FIFA Confederations Cup	**1** Brazilian Cup	**1** Recopa Sudamericana	
2 La Liga	**1** Spanish Super Cup	**1** FIFA Club World Cup	**1** Copa Libertadores	**1** Olympic Gold Medal	

STREET STAR

The son of a professional soccer player, Neymar was best friends with a ball from the age of two. He grew up playing street soccer and futsal, which helped him sharpen his skills and tricks. He was spotted by Santos FC and joined their youth team when he was only 11 years old and soon made a big impression as a dazzling forward and regular goal scorer. He almost signed for Real Madrid at the age of 14, but stayed with Santos for another five years, before switching to Spanish soccer in 2013 to join Catalan giants Barcelona.

BARÇA BOYS

In his four seasons at Camp Nou, Neymar formed part of what is considered by many to be the greatest strike force in soccer history. When the thrilling trio of Lionel Messi, Luis Suárez, and Neymar, nicknamed MSN, lined up together for Barça from 2013–17, the Catalan giant was almost unbeatable, winning an amazing nine trophies, including the domestic Treble in 2015. Neymar's individual stats for Barcelona are astonishing—105 goals scored and 59 assists in just 186 appearances.

MASSIVE MOVE

Following UEFA Champions League, La Liga, Spanish Cup, and FIFA Club World Cup wins with Barça, Neymar was ready to step out of Messi's shadow at the start of the 2017–18 season and take on a fresh challenge. Paris Saint-Germain triggered the mega $263 million release clause in Neymar's contract, handing him the number 10 shirt once worn by Zlatan Ibrahimović. He kicked off his PSG career in style, scoring 28 goals in his first 28 league matches!

Neymar scored his 50th international goal for Brazil against Argentina, aged just 24.

GAME FACT >>>>>

Neymar follows in the footsteps of Brazil legends Romário, Ronaldo, and Rivaldo, who all started out playing street soccer in bare feet. Neymar's heroes won four World Cups between them.

27

SERGIO RAMOS

Real Madrid's **FAMOUS NUMBER 4**, Sergio Ramos, captains both his country and his club side. The **CLASSY CENTER BACK** makes very few mistakes and loves to get forward. He's famous for scoring late goals despite the fact he's a center back! Ramos hit a **DOUBLE-FIGURE** goal tally for the first time in 2016–17, a season when Madrid won La Liga and the UEFA Champions League.

REAL MADRID

DEFENDER

FULL NAME:	Sergio Ramos García
NICKNAME:	Cuqui (Cookie)
DATE OF BIRTH:	March 30, 1986
PLACE OF BIRTH:	Camas, Spain
HEIGHT: 6 ft.	**WEIGHT:** 180 lbs.
LEFT OR RIGHT FOOTED:	Right
SQUAD NUMBER:	4
INTERNATIONAL TEAM:	Spain

STAT ATTACK

CLUBS

SEVILLA	REAL MADRID
Caps: 50 Goals 3	Caps: 548 Goals 70

TROPHIES

SEVILLA		REAL MADRID	
3 UEFA Champions League	**2** Spanish Cup	**3** UEFA Super Cup	**1** FIFA World Cup
4 La Liga	**3** Spanish Super Cup	**3** FIFA Club World Cup	**2** UEFA European Championship

SEVILLA START

Ramos didn't always dream of being a soccer player—his ambition was to be a bullfighter! Ramos's parents did not want him to get involved in such a dangerous sport. Instead, his brother encouraged him to try soccer and Ramos's natural talent was revealed. He joined Sevilla's youth team aged ten, and climbed the ranks until his first-team debut in February 2004. Ramos made 50 appearances for the club, where he showed he could play as both a ferocious fullback and a strong central defender. After three seasons at Sevilla, Ramos was a wanted man.

MADRID MOVE

Ramos moved to Madrid for over $30 million in 2005, a record for a Spanish teenager. Winning La Liga in 2007 was the first of an amazing 18 trophies with Real. 2016–17 was a brilliant season for Ramos—he led Real to a league and UEFA Champions League double, becoming the first man to captain his club to back-to-back Champions League wins. While Ramos is a fantastic defender, he has been sent off 24 times in total for Real (19 times in La Liga, which is a league record), though his reputation is for silly rather than deliberate fouls.

REIGNING FOR SPAIN

Ramos earned his first senior international cap just before turning 19, making him Spain's youngest player in 55 years. EURO 2008 was the first major tournament Ramos won with Spain, as the team entered a golden era of soccer. Made captain for the 2010 World Cup, Ramos started every game in South Africa, where Spain beat the Netherlands to be crowned World Champion. Another victorious tournament followed at EURO 2012. In 2013, he became Spain's youngest player to win 100 caps.

Ramos has enjoyed a glittering international career with Spain.

GAME FACT ▶▶▶▶

Ramos was once one of La Liga's fastest players and has clocked a sprinting speed of 19 miles per hour.

CRISTIANO
RONALDO

After winning a record-equaling **FIFTH BALLON D'OR** award in December 2017, Ronaldo has said he believes he is the **BEST PLAYER** in soccer history. An unstoppable forward, Ronaldo has a trophy cabinet that any soccer player would envy, having won over **20 CLUB TROPHIES**, the EURO 2016 title with Portugal, and a ton of individual awards—there are too many of Ron's records to mention!

REAL MADRID

FORWARD

FULL NAME:	Cristiano Ronaldo dos Santos Aveiro
NICKNAMES:	Ronnie, CR7
DATE OF BIRTH:	February 5, 1985
PLACE OF BIRTH:	Funchal, Madeira, Portugal
HEIGHT: 6 ft. 1 in.	**WEIGHT:** 185 lbs.
LEFT OR RIGHT FOOTED:	Both
SQUAD NUMBER:	7
INTERNATIONAL TEAM:	Portugal

STAT ATTACK

CLUBS

SPORTING CP B	SPORTING CP	MANCHESTER UNITED	REAL MADRID
Caps 2 Goals 0	Caps 31 Goals 5	Caps 292 Goals 118	Caps 423 Goals 431

TROPHIES

4 UEFA Champions League	**1** FA Cup	**1** FA Community Shield	**2** La Liga
1 UEFA European Championship	**3** Premier League	**2** English League Cup	**4** FIFA Club World Cup

2 Spanish Cup

2 Spanish Super Cup

2 UEFA Super Cup

TEENAGE SENSATION

Ronaldo made his first-team debut aged 17 at Sporting CP. But with a host of clubs interested in the young winger, he did not stay in Lisbon for long. A 2003 move to Manchester United for around $19 million made him the most expensive teenager in English soccer history at the time. There, he was given the number 7 shirt, which was available following David Beckham's transfer to Real Madrid. During his time at United, Ronaldo tore up English football—the goals flowed and his top-scoring season was 2007–08, when his 42 goals helped the Red Devils to the UEFA Champions League title, as well as the second of the three league titles Ronaldo won with the club.

FIRST-CLASS FORWARD

Hungry for more honors, Ronaldo moved to Real Madrid for a then world-record fee of $130 million. His debut season ended without a trophy, but Ronaldo still scored 33 goals. Since then he has won back-to-back UEFA Champions Leagues, two La Liga titles, and been named as the world's best player. Being able to score with either foot, his head, and from set pieces saw Ronaldo rack up a jaw-dropping 61 goals in 2014–15. He can create goals, too, and holds the record for the all-time number of assists in the UEFA Champions League, a competition in which he has scored over 100 goals.

CAPTAIN CRISTIANO

Ronaldo earned his first senior cap for Portugal aged 18 and made the EURO 2004 squad a year later. It was the first of eight major tournaments in which Ronaldo has appeared. One day after his 22nd birthday, in February 2007, Ronaldo captained Portugal for the first time, a role that he still holds. His 50th international goal made him the first Portuguese to play and score in three World Cups, and he is now easily the country's all-time top scorer with 79 goals. Ronaldo's biggest achievement with Portugal was to captain the side to its first ever victory in a major tournament at EURO 2016 in France.

As well as being Portugal's leading scorer, Ronaldo is the country's most capped player.

GAME FACT ⟫⟫⟫⟫

Ronaldo is so famous that he even has an airport named after him in Madeira, Portugal, the island where he grew up.

LUIS SUÁREZ

A stunning striker, Suárez has an unbelievable record of career goals with over **350 STRIKES** for five clubs in four different countries—wherever he's played he's scored! His journey from sweeping the streets in Uruguay to earn money for his family, to becoming one of **BARCELONA'S BEST**, reads like a soccer fairy tale. He's a **TRUE LEGEND** of the game.

BARCELONA

FORWARD

FULL NAME: Luis Alberto Suárez Díaz

NICKNAME: El Pistolero (the Pistol)

DATE OF BIRTH: January 24, 1987

PLACE OF BIRTH: Salto, Uruguay

HEIGHT: 5 ft. 11 in. **WEIGHT:** 189 lbs.

LEFT OR RIGHT FOOTED: Right

SQUAD NUMBER: 9

INTERNATIONAL TEAM: Uruguay

CLUBS	NACIONAL	GRONINGEN	AJAX	LIVERPOOL	BARCELONA
Caps	34	37	159	133	176
Goals	12	15	111	82	140

TROPHIES				
1 Uruguayan Primera División	1 Dutch Cup	2 La Liga	1 Spanish Super Cup	1 UEFA Super Cup
1 Dutch Eredivisie	1 English League Cup	3 Spanish Cup	1 UEFA Champions League	1 FIFA Club World Cup

TOUGH CHILDHOOD

Suárez is from Uruguay, a country with just 3.5 million people and where soccer brings the nation together. He began playing barefoot on the cobbled streets of his hometown, Salto. His family was poor, and Suárez did not even have his own soccer cleats. His tough start in life made him hungry for success. He won the league with Nacional aged 19, before being snapped up by Dutch club Groningen. After a single season there, Ajax made a move for the forward and Suárez went on to star for the Amsterdam club for three and a half seasons.

BEST FORM

Since his $110 million move to Barcelona in 2014, Suárez has gone from strength to strength. He won a league and UEFA Champions League double in his first season at the Nou Camp and contributed 25 goals and 20 assists in all competitions. Before Neymar left for PSG, Suárez, Messi, and Neymar formed perhaps the deadliest attacking trio in soccer history. In his first 100 matches for Barcelona, Suárez scored more goals and made more assists in Spain than both Cristiano Ronaldo and Lionel Messi managed in the same number of games—that's some record!

Suárez is a real team player, as shown by his five goals and seven assists in qualifying for Russia 2018.

REDS CAREER

Suárez joined Liverpool in January 2011 for around $35 million and was given the legendary number 7 shirt. By May 2013 he had established himself as one of Europe's top strikers and scored 30 goals that season. The following season was better still, when the Reds finished as runner-up in the Premier League. Suárez scored an incredible 31 goals in 37 matches, winning the Premier League Golden Boot and the Player of the Season award. The ambitious forward left Liverpool having scored 82 goals, but with only the League Cup trophy to show for his efforts.

GAME FACT ⟩⟩⟩⟩⟩

While Suárez is a talented soccer player, he has a bad-boy reputation. His long bans have taken some of the shine off a brilliant career.

DANI ALVES

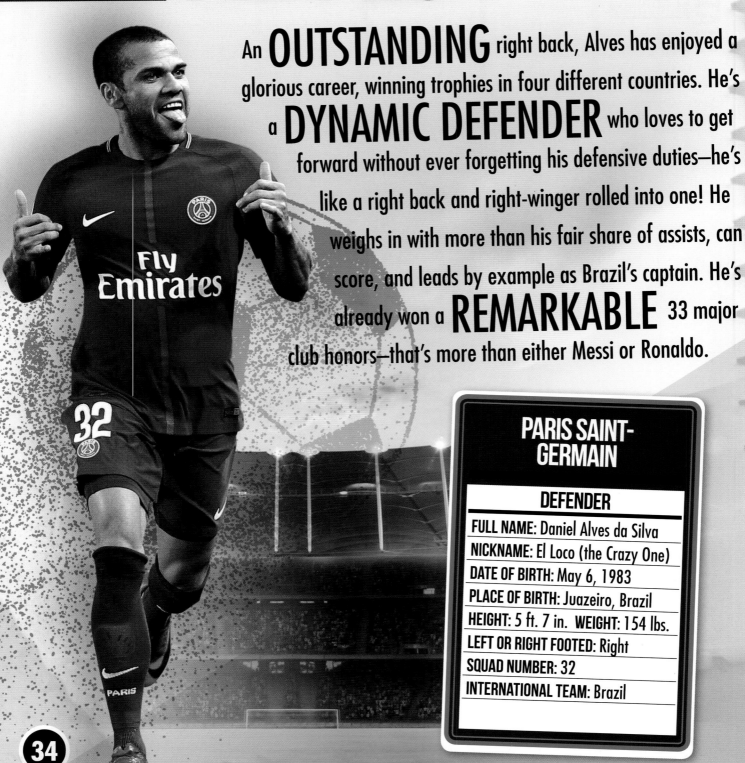

An **OUTSTANDING** right back, Alves has enjoyed a glorious career, winning trophies in four different countries. He's a **DYNAMIC DEFENDER** who loves to get forward without ever forgetting his defensive duties—he's like a right back and right-winger rolled into one! He weighs in with more than his fair share of assists, can score, and leads by example as Brazil's captain. He's already won a **REMARKABLE** 33 major club honors—that's more than either Messi or Ronaldo.

PARIS SAINT-GERMAIN

DEFENDER

FULL NAME: Daniel Alves da Silva

NICKNAME: El Loco (the Crazy One)

DATE OF BIRTH: May 6, 1983

PLACE OF BIRTH: Juazeiro, Brazil

HEIGHT: 5 ft. 7 in.   **WEIGHT:** 154 lbs.

LEFT OR RIGHT FOOTED: Right

SQUAD NUMBER: 32

INTERNATIONAL TEAM: Brazil

STAT ATTACK

CLUBS

	BAHIA	SEVILLA	BARCELONA	JUVENTUS	PARIS SAINT-GERMAIN
Caps	31	250	391	33	28
Goals	4	16	21	6	4

TROPHIES

BAHIA	SEVILLA	BARCELONA	JUVENTUS	PARIS SAINT-GERMAIN
3 UEFA Champ. League	4 UEFA Super Cup	5 Spanish Cup	3 FIFA Club World Cup	1 Italian Cup
1 Bahia Championship	2 UEFA Cup	6 La Liga	5 Spanish Super Cup	1 Serie A
				1 Copa América
				1 French Super Cup
				2 FIFA Confed. Cup

BIG DREAMS

Alves grew up in the state of Bahia, a poor, rural area in the northeast of Brazil. One of five children, Dani helped his father farm fruit growing up, though from a young age he dreamed of playing in a World Cup. After two seasons playing for local side Bahia, the defender moved to Spanish club Sevilla, where an impressive loan spell soon earned him a permanent deal with the La Liga club. Two UEFA Cup wins and a Spanish Cup victory with Sevilla kicked off his medal haul in Europe.

EUROPEAN GLORY

Alves transferred to Barcelona in 2008 for an initial fee of over $40 million, and with a reputation as one of the best fullbacks in the world. An amazing eight-season spell with Barça saw Dani win La Liga six times, the Spanish Cup four times, and the UEFA Champions League three times. Alves spent the 2016–17 season with Italian giant Juventus, arriving on a free transfer. He won the Serie A title along with the Italian Cup that year with Juve, but was on the move again the following season, signing a two-year deal with French superclub Paris Saint-Germain.

NATIONAL PRIDE

Alves has over 100 caps for Brazil, his first coming against Ecuador in 2006. His international highlights include the 2007 Copa América final against Argentina, where Alves scored the third goal in a 3–0 victory, plus FIFA Confederations Cup wins in 2009 and 2013. However, Alves and Brazil could only manage a disappointing fourth place in the 2014 FIFA World Cup on home turf. With the Brazil captaincy being rotated among senior squad members, Alves has pulled on the skipper's armband on more than one occasion.

Experienced Alves is one of the best fullbacks of his generation, and shows little sign of slowing down.

GAME FACT »»»»

Dani Alves was a key figure in helping to bring international teammate and best friend Neymar to PSG.

KEYLOR NAVAS

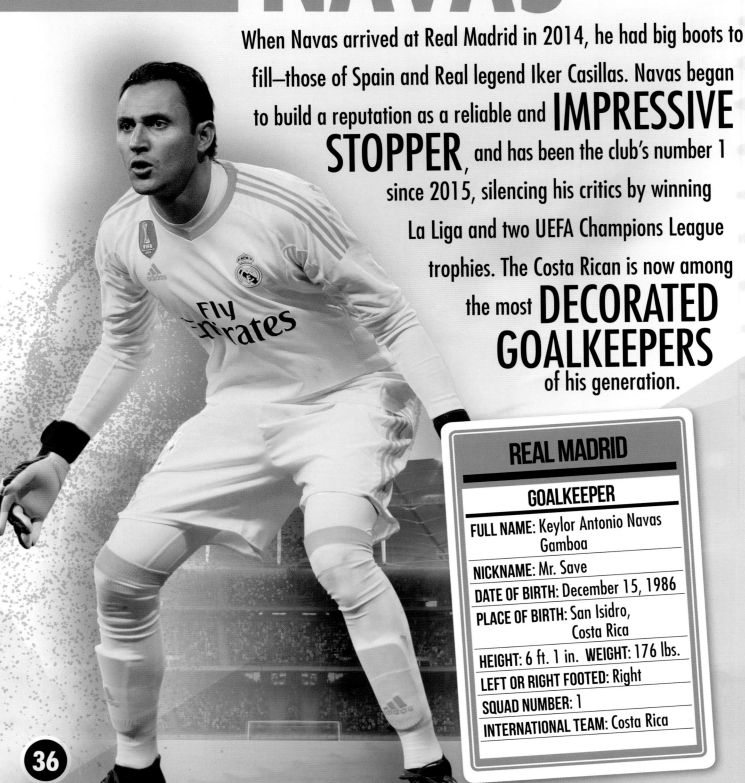

When Navas arrived at Real Madrid in 2014, he had big boots to fill—those of Spain and Real legend Iker Casillas. Navas began to build a reputation as a reliable and **IMPRESSIVE STOPPER**, and has been the club's number 1 since 2015, silencing his critics by winning La Liga and two UEFA Champions League trophies. The Costa Rican is now among the most **DECORATED GOALKEEPERS** of his generation.

REAL MADRID

GOALKEEPER

FULL NAME:	Keylor Antonio Navas Gamboa
NICKNAME:	Mr. Save
DATE OF BIRTH:	December 15, 1986
PLACE OF BIRTH:	San Isidro, Costa Rica
HEIGHT: 6 ft. 1 in.	**WEIGHT:** 176 lbs.
LEFT OR RIGHT FOOTED:	Right
SQUAD NUMBER:	1
INTERNATIONAL TEAM:	Costa Rica

STAT ATTACK

CLUBS

DEPORTIVO SAPRISSA	ALBACETE BALOMPIÉ	LEVANTE	REAL MADRID
Caps 52	Caps 36	Caps 70	Caps 123
Goals 0	Goals 0	Goals 0	Goals 0

TROPHIES

1 La Liga **2** UEFA Champions League **3** FIFA Club World Cup **1** CONCACAF Champions League

1 Spanish Super Cup **2** UEFA Super Cup **6** Costa Rican Primera División

RURAL ROOTS

Keylor Navas was born to working-class parents in San Isidro, a rural town in the south of Costa Rica. After his parents emigrated to the United States, Navas was raised by his grandfather. At the age of 14 the young keeper secured a trial with Deportivo Saprissa, one of Costa Rica's biggest clubs. The club recognized Navas's qualities and he went on to win six domestic league titles and the CONCACAF Champions League, before moving to Albacete Balompié in the Spanish second division.

GOLDEN GLOVES

A first international cap for Navas came in October 2008 in a World Cup qualifier, though Costa Rica fell short of reaching South Africa 2010. Navas's World Cup debut was to come in 2014 as Costa Rica reached the quarterfinals for the first time ever, with the keeper in superb form. He was nominated for the Golden Glove Award for the tournament's best keeper, having achieved three shutouts. Navas was part of the Costa Rican squad at the 2018 FIFA World Cup in Russia, when the country made its fifth appearance in the finals.

Navas enjoys almost superhero status in his home country of Costa Rica.

RISE TO THE TOP

Relegation for Albacete in Navas's first season saw him loaned to La Liga club Levante. He established himself as Levante's first-choice keeper in 2013–14, and was named La Liga's best stopper that season. A string of outstanding performances for Costa Rica at the 2014 World Cup saw Navas join Real Madrid for around $13 million. While Real is regularly linked to the world's top keepers, manager Zinedine Zidane has shown great faith in the consistent Navas, who has now played over 100 games for Los Blancos.

GAME FACT »»»»»

Navas almost signed for Manchester United in 2015 in a deal that would have seen David de Gea move to Madrid. The deal fell through when the paperwork missed the deadline.

DAVID DE GEA

Manchester United and Spain goalkeeper de Gea is one of world soccer's **TOP STOPPERS**. He rose through the ranks at Atlético Madrid to become the club's **NUMBER 1** at the age of just 18. This tall, athletic keeper has outstanding agility, composure, and speed in his locker. His **SPECTACULAR** saves for Manchester United saw him voted the Red Devils' player of the year three times in a row.

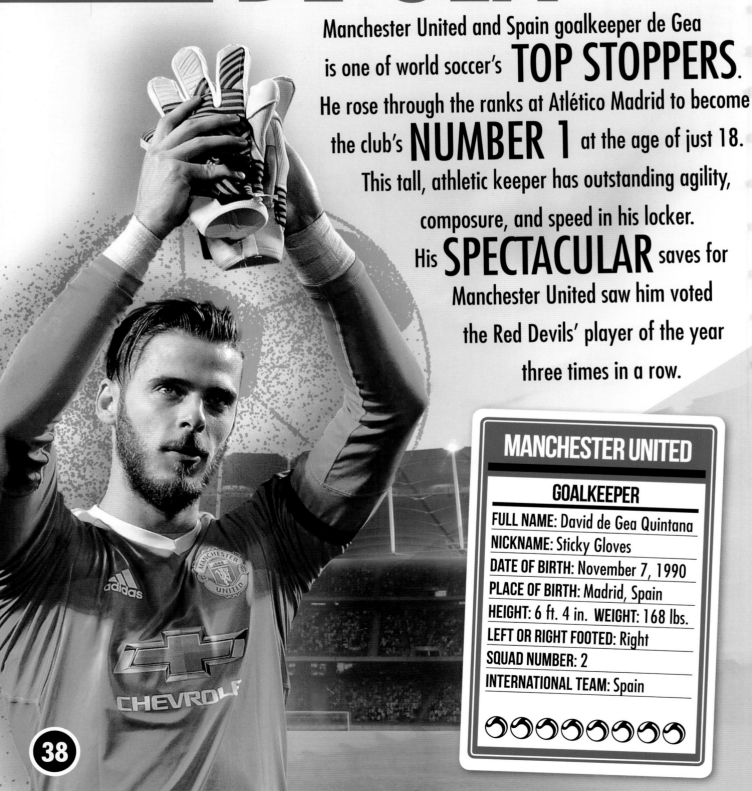

MANCHESTER UNITED

GOALKEEPER

FULL NAME: David de Gea Quintana

NICKNAME: Sticky Gloves

DATE OF BIRTH: November 7, 1990

PLACE OF BIRTH: Madrid, Spain

HEIGHT: 6 ft. 4 in. WEIGHT: 168 lbs.

LEFT OR RIGHT FOOTED: Right

SQUAD NUMBER: 2

INTERNATIONAL TEAM: Spain

CLUBS		
ATLÉTICO MADRID B	ATLÉTICO MADRID	MANCHESTER UNITED
Caps 35	Caps 84	Caps 301
Goals 0	Goals 0	Goals 0

TROPHIES **1** Premier League **1** FA Cup **1** English League Cup **3** FA Community Shield **2** UEFA Europa League **1** UEFA Super Cup

SURPRISING START

Goalkeeper de Gea joined Atlético Madrid's academy at the age of 13, although he had previously starred as a striker growing up. He was as good at scoring goals as he was keeping them out! In de Gea's debut season for Atlético's first team, he played a key role in winning the UEFA Europa League—the club's first major European trophy in almost 50 years. A UEFA Super Cup victory against Inter Milan followed, as the cool-headed keeper kept out a 90th-minute penalty.

FROM MADRID TO MANCHESTER

In the summer of 2011, Manchester United paid a reported $30 million for de Gea, a British record fee for a goalkeeper at the time. The young Spaniard endured a tough start at the club in his first season, though as his confidence and reputation grew, he managed 11 shutouts and won a Premier League medal in the following campaign. He has since added a second UEFA Europa League title, as well as English FA and League Cup victories, to his trophy cabinet, while achieving over 100 shutouts for United.

SPANISH STAR

De Gea helped Spain's under-17 team win the 2007 UEFA European Championship, and finish as runner-up at the FIFA U-17 World Cup in the same year. A few years later, he was part of the squad that won the 2011 UEFA European Under-21 Championship, and a second European crown was successfully defended in 2013. He was called up to Spain's senior side for the 2014 World Cup, but did not make an appearance. It was at EURO 2016 that de Gea was to establish himself as his country's number 1, ahead of legendary keeper Iker Casillas.

De Gea took over goalkeeping duties from Iker Casillas, one of Spanish soccer's greatest ever players.

GAME FACT ⟫⟫⟫

De Gea is the only Manchester United player to have been voted the club's Player of the Year three times in a row.

39

LUKA MODRIĆ

Croatia's classy captain Luka Modrić is one of the **BEST CENTRAL MIDFIELDERS** in world soccer. While his teammates such as Ronaldo hit the headlines, Modrić quietly protects his defense, supplying inch-perfect balls and **SURGING FORWARD** to join the Madrid attack line, too. The midfielder is at the hub of Los Blancos, and has the silverware to show for it. Even after six seasons at the Bernabéu, he's as hungry for trophies as when he first arrived in Spain.

REAL MADRID

MIDFIELDER

FULL NAME: Luka Modrić

NICKNAME: Lucky Luka

DATE OF BIRTH: September 9, 1985

PLACE OF BIRTH: Zadar, SFR Yugoslavia

HEIGHT: 5 ft. 8 in. **WEIGHT:** 145 lbs.

LEFT OR RIGHT FOOTED: Both

SQUAD NUMBER: 10

INTERNATIONAL TEAM: Croatia

CLUBS				
DINAMO ZAGREB	HŠK ZRINJSKI MOSTAR (LOAN)	INTER ZAPREŠIĆ (LOAN)	TOTTENHAM HOTSPUR	REAL MADRID
Caps 128	Caps 22	Caps 18	Caps 159	Caps 244
Goals 32	Goals 8	Goals 4	Goals 17	Goals 13

TROPHIES				
	1 Spanish Cup	3 UEFA Champions League	3 UEFA Super Cup	2 Croatian Cup
1 La Liga	2 Spanish Super Cup	2 FIFA Club World Cup	3 Croatian League	1 Croatian Super Cup

CHILDHOOD CONFLICT

Modrić was born in northern Dalmatia in Croatia at a time of conflict. When the Croatian War of Independence worsened in 1991, his family was forced to flee its home and become refugees, staying in a hotel in nearby Zadar. The young Luka was rarely without a ball at his feet and, aged seven, he joined Zadar's youth setup, where he impressed with his superb ball control. At 16, Croatia's top club, Dinamo Zagreb, came calling, though it would take two loan spells at smaller clubs before Modrić grew into one of the country's most gifted young players.

BIG IMPRESSION

A big-money move was only a matter of time. Barcelona was interested, but the English Premier League proved to be Modrić's destination. The midfielder signed for Tottenham Hotspur for a club record of over $35 million in 2008. Despite a quiet first campaign and a broken leg in his second season, Modrić went on to become one of Spurs' all-time great midfielders. London rival Chelsea pulled out all the stops to poach him, but it was Real Madrid that secured Modrić's services next, in a move worth around $42 million.

MADRID'S MAESTRO

While fans didn't warm to the little midfielder straightaway, Modrić worked hard to guarantee his starting place under a succession of managers at Madrid. He has since won La Liga, the Spanish Cup, and the UEFA Champions League (an incredible three times), as well as two Club World Cups. Real depends on his quality and consistency—he pulls the strings from midfield to control games, delivers set pieces with deadly accuracy, and unlocks defenses with ease.

Modrić has been voted Croatia's player of the year six times.

GAME FACT ≫≫≫≫

Modrić was voted the world's fifth best soccer player at the Ballon d'Or awards in 2017. He was also the highest ranking midfielder.

41

YOUNG GUNS

OUSMANE DEMBÉLÉ

DEMBÉLÉ ADDS PACE AND POWER TO BARCELONA'S ATTACK.

Barcelona believed Dembélé to be one of the game's hottest prospects and brought him in for a fee of around $130 million to replace Neymar—making him the second most expensive player in history along with Paul Pogba. The young forward has pace and can use both feet to devastating effect when fully fit. Unfortunately, injury limited his appearances in his debut La Liga season.

BARCELONA

FORWARD

DATE OF BIRTH: May 15, 1997	
PLACE OF BIRTH: Vernon, France	
HEIGHT: 5 ft. 10 in. **WEIGHT:** 161 lbs.	
LEFT OR RIGHT FOOTED: Both	
SQUAD NUMBER: 11	
INTERNATIONAL TEAM: France	
DOMESTIC APPEARANCES: 109; **GOALS:** 35	

GIANLUIGI DONNARUMMA

THIS YOUNG ITALIAN KEEPER HAS A BRIGHT FUTURE IN THE GAME.

Donnarumma debuted for AC Milan's first team as a 16-year-old—almost unheard of for a keeper! He achieved 31 shutouts in his first 92 Serie A matches and made a penalty shoot-out save to secure the club's first trophy in five seasons—the 2016 Italian Super Cup. Now Gianluigi Buffon has retired from international soccer, Italy's number 1 shirt should easily belong to Donnarumma.

AC MILAN

GOALKEEPER

DATE OF BIRTH: February 25, 1999	
PLACE OF BIRTH: Castellammare di Stabia, Italy	
HEIGHT: 6 ft. 5 in. **WEIGHT:** 198 lbs.	
LEFT OR RIGHT FOOTED: Right	
SQUAD NUMBER: 99	
INTERNATIONAL TEAM: Italy	
DOMESTIC APPEARANCES: 106	

Now you know which players made the grade as the superstars of world soccer, it's time to showcase the skills of the next generation. Big things are predicted for these youngsters over the next decade, with some of them already starring for club and country. Take a look at our selection of top talent, from a commanding keeper to some sensational strikers.

CHRISTIAN PULISIC

A SPEEDY MIDFIELDER WHO CAN PLAY ON EITHER WING.

Could this teenager be the USA's best ever player? He's already played over 50 games in the Bundesliga and is Borussia Dortmund's youngest scorer in the UEFA Champions League. Cool under pressure, he can use both feet and may very well be the first world-class player to come out of the States. The fact that the U.S. failed to qualify for the 2018 FIFA World Cup will only drive Pulisic's ambition.

BORUSSIA DORTMUND

MIDFIELDER

DATE OF BIRTH: September 18, 1998

PLACE OF BIRTH: Hershey, Pennsylvania, USA

HEIGHT: 5 ft. 8 in. **WEIGHT:** 139 lbs.

LEFT OR RIGHT FOOTED: Both

SQUAD NUMBER: 22

INTERNATIONAL TEAM: USA

DOMESTIC APPEARANCES: 82; **GOALS:** 11

JADON SANCHO

TEENAGER SANCHO WEARS THE NUMBER 7 SHIRT FOR DORTMUND.

Winger Sancho was in the England U17 squad that won the World Cup in 2017. He was also crowned player of the tournament for his performances in the UEFA European U17 Championship earlier that year. He moved to Borussia Dortmund from Manchester City in search of first-team soccer and could be destined for great things in Germany.

BORUSSIA DORTMUND

ATTACKING MIDFIELDER

DATE OF BIRTH: March 25, 2000

PLACE OF BIRTH: London, England

HEIGHT: 5 ft. 10 in. **WEIGHT:** 167 lbs.

LEFT OR RIGHT FOOTED: Right

SQUAD NUMBER: 7

INTERNATIONAL TEAM: England

DOMESTIC APPEARANCES: 9; **GOALS:** 0

YOUNG GUNS

THEO HERNÁNDEZ

Real Madrid's classy French left back Theo Hernández is known simply as Theo. He moved across Madrid to join Los Blancos from Atlético in the summer of 2017 and made a handful of appearances in defense in his first season, as well as winning two trophies—the Spanish and UEFA Super Cups. His dream is to play for France's senior side, although he may be tempted by a call-up from Spain if one comes.

REAL MADRID

DEFENDER

DATE OF BIRTH: October 6, 1997

PLACE OF BIRTH: Marseille, France

HEIGHT: 6 ft. **WEIGHT:** 176 lbs.

LEFT OR RIGHT FOOTED: Left

SQUAD NUMBER: 15

INTERNATIONAL TEAM: France

DOMESTIC APPEARANCES: 63; **GOALS:** 2

DELE ALLI

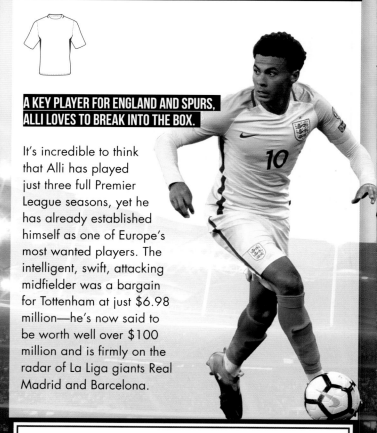

It's incredible to think that Alli has played just three full Premier League seasons, yet he has already established himself as one of Europe's most wanted players. The intelligent, swift, attacking midfielder was a bargain for Tottenham at just $6.98 million—he's now said to be worth well over $100 million and is firmly on the radar of La Liga giants Real Madrid and Barcelona.

TOTTENHAM HOTSPUR

ATTACKING MIDFIELDER

DATE OF BIRTH: April 11, 1996

PLACE OF BIRTH: Milton Keynes, England

HEIGHT: 6 ft. 2 in. **WEIGHT:** 175 lbs.

LEFT OR RIGHT FOOTED: Right

SQUAD NUMBER: 20

INTERNATIONAL TEAM: England

DOMESTIC APPEARANCES: 217; **GOALS:** 65

PIETRO PELLEGRI

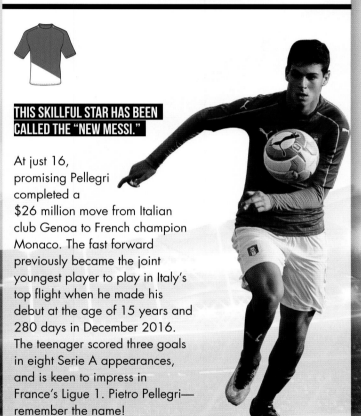

THIS SKILLFUL STAR HAS BEEN CALLED THE "NEW MESSI."

At just 16, promising Pellegri completed a $26 million move from Italian club Genoa to French champion Monaco. The fast forward previously became the joint youngest player to play in Italy's top flight when he made his debut at the age of 15 years and 280 days in December 2016. The teenager scored three goals in eight Serie A appearances, and is keen to impress in France's Ligue 1. Pietro Pellegri—remember the name!

AS MONACO

FORWARD

DATE OF BIRTH: March 17, 2001	
PLACE OF BIRTH: Genoa, Italy	
HEIGHT: 6 ft. 2 in.	**WEIGHT:** 176 lbs.
LEFT OR RIGHT FOOTED: Right	
SQUAD NUMBER: 23	
INTERNATIONAL TEAM: Italy	
DOMESTIC APPEARANCES: 10;	**GOALS:** 3

THE BENCH

These super substitutes complete our Young Guns squad.

DAVINSON SÁNCHEZ
Tottenham & Colombia
defender

JUSTIN KLUIVERT
Ajax midfielder

YOURI TIELEMANS
Anderlecht & Belgium
midfielder

FEDERICO CHIESA
Fiorentina midfielder

BEN WOODBURN
Liverpool & Wales
forward

ALL-STARS QUIZ

LOOK BACK THROUGH THE BOOK IF YOU GET STUCK.

Try this **ALL-STARS QUIZ** on your own or with another soccer fan to see who's top of the league. The answers are at the bottom of the page, but don't peek until you've finished answering all the questions.

1 Which player does not play international soccer for the "Red Devils"?
A Kevin De Bruyne ○
B Manuel Neuer ○
C Eden Hazard ○

2 Whose nickname is "El Loco"?
A Luis Suárez ○
B Lionel Messi ○
C Dani Alves ○

3 Who is the only goalkeeper to feature in the Young Guns section?
A Manuel Neuer ○
B Gianluigi Donnarumma ○
C Jadon Sancho ○

4 Which two players have won the Ballon d'Or prize a record five times each?
A Lionel Messi and Neymar ○
B Luis Suárez and Lionel Messi ○
C Lionel Messi and Cristiano Ronaldo ○

5 What is the nickname of Barcelona's one-time legendary attacking force?
A MSN ○
B FCB ○
C The fearsome threesome ○

6 For which national team does Luis Suárez play?
A Brazil ○
B Chile ○
C Uruguay ○

7 In which position does Marcelo play for Real Madrid?
A Defense ○
B Midfield ○
C Attack ○

8 Goalkeeper Manuel Neuer began his career at which German club?
A VfB Stuttgart ○
B Hannover 96 ○
C Schalke 04 ○

9 What number does Harry Kane wear on the back of his shirt for Tottenham?

A 9 ○
B 10 ○
C 18 ○

10 Luka Modrić plays soccer for which international team?

A Russia ○
B Norway ○
C Croatia ○

11 Which Superstar is so famous that he has an airport named after him?

A Robert Lewandowski ○
B Cristiano Ronaldo ○
C Dani Alves ○

12 Keeper Keylor Navas plays for which international team?

A Chile ○
B Costa Rica ○
C United States ○

13 Which of these Superstars is not a FIFA World Cup winner?

A Andrés Iniesta ○
B Leonardo Bonucci ○
C Toni Kroos ○

14 Who is the only Polish player among our Superstars selection?

A Toni Kroos ○
B Robert Lewandowski ○
C Luka Modrić ○

15 Whose transfer in 2017 made him the world's most expensive player?

A Cristiano Ronaldo ○
B Ousmane Dembélé ○
C Neymar ○

16 Which Superstar has played for both AC Milan and Juventus?

A Gianluigi Donnarumma ○
B Dani Alves ○
C Leonardo Bonucci ○

17 Who is the only player from the United States to feature in this book?

A Landon Donovan ○
B Christian Pulisic ○
C Jozy Altidore ○

18 Which famous forward has netted over 500 times for one club?

A Cristiano Ronaldo ○
B Robert Lewandowski ○
C Lionel Messi ○

19 Which FIFA World Cup winner is known as "the Illusionist"?

A Manuel Neuer ○
B Andrés Iniesta ○
C Toni Kroos ○

20 Which Superstar's childhood ambition was to become a bullfighter when he grew up?

A Leonardo Bonucci ○
B Sergio Ramos ○
C Marcelo ○

QUIZ ANSWERS 1. B – Manuel Neuer; 2. C – Dani Alves; 3. B – Gianluigi Donnarumma; 4. C – Lionel Messi and Cristiano Ronaldo; 5. A – MSN (Messi, Suárez, Neymar); 6. C – Uruguay; 7. A – Defense; 8. C – Schalke 04; 9. B – 10; 10. C – Croatia; 11. B – Cristiano Ronaldo; 12. B – Costa Rica; 13. B – Leonardo Bonucci; 14. B – Robert Lewandowski; 15. C – Neymar; 16. C – Leonardo Bonucci; 17. B – Christian Pulisic; 18. C – Lionel Messi; 19. B – Andrés Iniesta; 20. B – Sergio Ramos.

47

PICTURE CREDITS

The publishers would like to thank the following sources for their kind permission to reproduce the pictures in this book.

Getty Images: /Roberto Serra/Iguana Press: 45
REX/Shutterstock: /AFP7: 16, 20; /AP: 43R; /APA-PictureDesk GmbH: 18, 41; /Action Press: 1, 24; /Aflo: 6, 9, 29; /Nicolas Aguilera/EPA: 33; /Facundo Arrizabalaga/ EPA-EFE: 10; /Armando Babani/EPA-EFE: 43L; /Bagu Blanco: 7, 32; /Broadimage: 31; /Richard Calver: 35; /Sergei Chirikov/EPA-EFE: 23; /Manu Fernandez/AP: 2; /Foto Olimpik/Sipa USA: 19; /Hollandse Hoogte: 4-5, 11, 22, 40; /Guillaume Horcajuelo/ EPA-EFE: 26; /Alex James/JMP: 21, 38; /Rodrigo Jimenez/EPA-EFE: 30, 44L; /James March/BPI: 25; /Paul Marriott: 15; /Kieran McManus/BPI: 12; /Matt McNulty/JMP: 8; /Rob Noyes/Digital South/SilverHub: 44R; /Andre Penner/AP: 27; /Pixathlon: 13, 36, 39; /Adam Rivers/ProSports: 28; /Robbie Stephenson/JMP: 14; /VW Pics/ZUMA: 37; /Yoan Valat/EPA-EFE: 34; /Friedemann Vogel/EPA-EFE: 17; /Michael Zemanek: 42L; /Michael Zemanek/BPI: 42R
Shutterstock: Max Bukovski, Evgeni Matrosov and Youimages: backgrounds